The Lives and Reigns of the Holy Roman Emperors

Rich Callaghan

Published by Rich Callaghan, 2023.

THE LIVES AND REIGNS OF THE HOLY ROMAN EMPERORS

First edition. January 11, 2023.

Copyright © 2023 Rich Callaghan.

ISBN: 979-8215806067

Written by Rich Callaghan.

Charlemagne's date of birth is not completely clear but it is generally accepted to be around 747. Likewise, there is some doubt over his place of birth. However, the remains in his tomb at Aachen are believed in fact to be those of the man himself and historians have suggested this could also have been where he was born too. Charlemagne's rise to be one of the most significant figures in early medieval European history is not a complete surprise considering his family pedigree. He was the grandson of Charles Martel or Charles the Hammer.

Martel himself was an extraordinary man. Islam was very much on the march in Europe during the 8th century conquering virtually all of Spain and was now on the doorstep of the Franks. It was only thanks to Martel's brutal victory at the Battle of Tours in 732 that halted the march of the Muslims and saved the Christian west from further assaults. Charles Martel was an uncompromising type and he put an end to any tyrannic rule in Frankish territory.

Charlemagne's father died in 768 and he and his brother Carloman divided the succession between them. Carloman didn't last long however and he died just two years later and Charlemagne was elevated to king of the Franks around 770.

His first duty was to put a swift end to troublesome areas in his kingdom. There was an uprising in Aquitaine which was put down quickly with a combination of diplomacy and a threat of force. Then, after a difficult progress into Italy via the Alps, he put down further trouble in the Lombard region using siege warfare and bringing Italy into line.

His biggest problem in the early years of his reign as king was putting an end to the Frankish war with the Saxons which had dragged on for decades. The Saxons had been defeated on countless occasions and brought to terms but any time they were, they would almost instantly go back on their word and cause further trouble for the Frankish kings and their people. Charlemagne's dealings with the Saxons in Germany continued until the early 9th century when he put an end to the war by splitting up the Saxon tribes and resettled in different regions across his kingdom. Charlemagne led various other campaigns where he put down uprisings as swiftly as they had arisen.

It's worth mentioning here that although Charlemagne was a fantastic military leader, it would be easy to assume that family was completely secondary to him but that was not the case. As a father, he was very close to his children and took them with him on his campaigns. Charlemagne avoided marrying off his daughters despite it being custom at the time to do so. Whether this was because of his love for his children or for other reasons, it can only be speculated.

His success militarily continued, defeating the Huns in a campaign led largely by his son Pepin which proved to be a shrewd decision by the king as the Franks suffered very little damage in the war.

Charlemagne's influence was widespread. He had diplomatic relations with King Offa (757-796) of the Mercians. Relations appeared to be good although Offa seems to have overstepped the mark with the Frankish king when he proposed a marriage between his son and Charlemagne's daughter. This obviously irritated Charlemagne who broke off ties in 790 although things were patched up enough for them to conclude a treaty in 795.

In what would have been one of the most extraordinary events in medieval history was when marriage was proposed to Charlemagne himself. The offer came from the Byzantine Empress Irene. Irene was a self serving and brutal woman, blinding her own son Constantine VI, which eventually killed him, and seized power for herself. Marrying Charlemagne would have not only increased her prestige but also secured her position which would have been extremely vulnerable as not only a murdering usurper but as a woman as well. Ultimately the match didn't happen and Irene lost power in 802. Relations with the Byzantine empire didn't end with Irene and the following emperors also sought an alliance with the now Holy Roman Emperor, a title that the Eastern Roman Empire didn't particularly approve of.

Which brings us onto the story of his being crowned Holy Roman Emperor by Pope Leo III. Being Pope around the 8th, 9th and 10th centuries could be a particularly unpleasant experience. Stories of popes being usurped, murdered or having rival popes installed against them (anti popes) were rife and Leo's story is no less brutal, having been blinded and his tongue torn out by the citizens of Rome. Charlemagne went to his aid where Leo offered to crown him Emperor. Charlemagne put on a show of being reluctant to accept but the ceremony went ahead and the institution of Holy Roman Empire had been born and would last a millennium.

As I mentioned, the news of this did not go down particularly well in Constantinople and the Byzantine empire. The Byzantines saw themselves as the true continuation of the fallen Western Roman Empire, which had ended in the 5th century, and the elevation of Charles was seen as a threat to their position. However, the fact that alliances continued to be sought in the east with Charlemagne shows how high his standing was as a brilliant military leader, king and now Emperor.

By the time of his accession, Charlemagne would have been in his 50s. For his time, he had already reached a good age. Time now to think about the future and in 813, he had his son Louis the Pious crowned co emperor alongside him. The crowning of co rulers had been particularly common in the Eastern Roman Empire and would continue through European medieval history. When he died a year later, Charlemagne had his affairs in order and his legacy totally secure as one of the brilliant kings in all history.

Louis the Pious became co Emperor in 813 alongside his father Charlemagne who had been crowned the first Holy Roman Emperor in 800 by Pope Leo III. When his father died the following year, Louis' reign seemed to be going well and could have in fact been classed as successful up until 830 when his sons would revolt and he would have a particularly turbulent relationship with his son Lothair and would even be captive to him twice, although he eventually regained power both times.

Louis was born in the late 770s, probably 778. The chronicler Einhard, who wrote the life of Charlemagne, the best primary source about Charles the Great, touches upon the education of Charlemagne's children. Charlemagne was unusually close to his children and took them with him on campaigns rather than leaving them in the care of nobility where they might have been expected to receive their education. However, in the care of their mother and father, Louis and his siblings were taught to read and write. As they grew older, the boys were taught the skills that would be expected of them as princes and warriors such as learning to ride horses, the art of warfare such as handling weapons and going hunting, the favourite pastime of the nobility in the middle ages. The girls were predictably taught more domesticated skills such as cloth making.

Death was a common thing in the 8th and 9th centuries and Einhard mentions the death of three of Louis' siblings. Two brothers Charles and Pepin, the latter of whom might have been expected great things due to him successfully leading a military campaign on behalf of his father against the Huns with very little loss on the Frankish side. Louis also lost a sister, Hruodrud. Given there seems to have been a close bond between the children and their father, it's fair to say the losses would have been felt sorely. The death of these three siblings occurred before Charlemagne's death in 814. As I mentioned, death was commonplace throughout the Middle Ages and parents burying their children was not unusual though still a heavy blow even to one of the great warrior kings of the Age.

Unsurprisingly for someone nicknamed The Pious, Louis was a mild mannered man, described by William of Malmesbury as being "unmercifully persecuted " by his son Lothair inspired, according to William, by Louis' favouritism of Lothair's youngest brother, Charles and the handing of Germany to him . When Louis's father, Charlemagne died, Louis had been in Aquitaine when the message arrived to inform him he was now sole ruler. His succession went uncontested.

An important early boost for Louis was the forming of an alliance with Byzantine emperor Leo V, who was still relatively new on the throne himself. It was perhaps this that encouraged Leo to seek a friendship with the Emperor in the West. Byzantine history is full to the brim of deposed Emperors and rulers meeting a violent end. Securing a treaty with Louis would bolster his position. It was an agreement that would be mutually beneficial as, although during the 14 year reign of Charlemagne as Holy Roman Emperor there had been several attempts from the Eastern Roman Empire to secure agreements, the relations between the East and Western empires would not be easy throughout their histories so Louis and Leo coming to terms early in their reigns would suit both.

Things continued to go well for Louis. He obliged in helping two deposed Danish kings and he received homage from nobility throughout his kingdom. His next port of call was Rome where a plot had been uncovered against the Pope who had done the righteous and merciful thing you might have expected of a pope and promptly slaughtered his enemies. Eventually the situation calmed down. The papacy in the 9th century was always volatile and a bit like the situation with the Byzantine emperors, popes were very often opposed, sometimes deposed and occasionally met a violent end. Quickly calming down matters in Rome was crucial for Louis and peace in his kingdom.

In 816, Louis put down two further revolts, the first by the Slavs and the latter by the Basques. The latter had been frustrated by Louis' removal of their corrupt ruler but they were successfully dealt with by Louis' forces. Later that year, Louis met the new pope where they made an alliance. Again, Louis seems to have been fully aware of the importance of stability in Rome and making friendship with Pope Stephen was the wisest course of action.

In 817, Louis welcomed envoys to his court of the son of the Muslim ruler in Spain, seeking peace in the region and also that year, another envoy from Constantinople sought his advice on a dilemma for Leo V.

Louis had a fortunate escape when he was walking on an arcade, along with many others, which collapsed, killing and injuring many with the Emperor coming away with only bumps and bruises. Then, following in the custom of his father, Louis crowned his oldest son Lothair co Emperor and started the beginning of his troubles. Lothair would have been around 22 at the time of his coronation. A prince of this age would have been, or expected to be, itching for power. At the time of Lothair being made co Emperor, his brothers Pepin and Louis were given Aquitaine and Bavaria respectively with Lothair their overlord.

For the time being Louis continued to manage his kingdom. His nephew, the king of Italy, rose up in revolt which was swiftly put down and his son Pepin dealt with an uprising in Gascony. A problem of a different kind befell the Franks when a huge and persistent rainfall led to floods and the failing of crops and vegetables, leading to widespread hunger and starvation.

In 821, Lothair was married to the daughter of the Count of Tours before he was sent by his father to Worms. At this point, Lothair was still compliant to his father and, after dealing with matters in Italy, he went to meet the pope on behalf of Louis in 823. Before leaving Italy, Lothair established new laws which obviously gained the approval of his father who then sent a nobleman to enforce them.

Matters would continue in much the same vein up until 830. Lothair seemed to be a loyal co ruler, carrying out his father's wishes while other rulers such as the Bulgar khan continued to seek alliances with Louis.

But in 830, matters would turn against Louis. Whether Lothair had been fully loyal and felt genuinely aggrieved or whether he now, at the age of about 35, felt he had an opportunity to seize full control is difficult to say but to me, Lothair seems to have manufactured an uprising to suit his own ends and it seems to have also suited two of his other brothers, Pepin and Louis who rose in revolt also.

Their initial move was against their step mother and uncles who they forced into a convent and monastery respectively in Aquitaine, guarded by Pepin's men. Next, they took their father and brother prisoner albeit in kinder conditions with them even sending monks to keep Charles, at that time about 7 years old, company and possibly hoped he would then choose a religious life. That didn't come to fruition as he would go on to become Holy Roman Emperor too but he would have to continue his struggle even after the death of Louis the Pious.

However, the deposition was not successful and the governance went to pot. Louis was quickly restored to oversee matters. Chastised, Lothair had seen his followers who helped him with his coup either executed or exiled and he was once more sent to Italy. The situation kicked off again in 833 when Louis, through what can be considered pretty poor judgement in the circumstances, took Aquitaine off Pepin and gave it to Charles. Once more, he and his son found themselves captive.

Again, Lothair lost control of matters and spent his time in sole power squabbling with his brothers and other members of his following. Louis and Charles were once more released and Lothair did a runner. Acting more sensibly this time, Louis accepted Pepin's homage when he came back to his father and restored to him Aquitaine. Lothair continued to revolt up until the middle of 834 when eventually he saw he didn't have enough backing after the nobility had evidently grown fed up of what had been a largely needless civil war caused by weak kingship and a temperamental son.

When Louis died in 840, he must have been a tired and weary man. He would have been around 62 at the time of his death, a good age for the 9th century. Troublesome sons was not an uncommon matter in the early middle ages or throughout the entire Medieval period in fact. Louis had demonstrated good diplomatic skills and kept good control of his kingdom for over 15 years but to be deposed twice does show a weakness in his kingship. He had put down numerous revolts but seems to have had a weak spot when it came to his sons, Lothair in particular. Perhaps we can't be too hard on Louis as the headstrong Lothair would continue to quarrel with his brothers after he had become sole emperor.

Lothair I had caused his father no end of problems. In what had been a relatively stable reign up until about 830, Louis the Pious twice found himself deposed because of Lothair and two of his brothers, Pepin and Louis the German. Pepin perhaps had some right to feel aggrieved because his father had taken land off him and given it to the trios half brother, Charles. However, both times that Louis was deposed, Lothair found himself struggling to govern the kingdom and was both times forced to allow Louis to reassume authority. He eventually succeeded to full power when his father died in 840. Lothair's brother Pepin having died the previous year,

By the time of his succession in 840, Lothair would have been in his mid forties having been born about 795. A man of this age coming to the throne might have been expected to rule sensibly but Lothair seems to have been the quarrelsome type and would spend the first three years of his sole rule bickering with his remaining brothers. Louis the German had been born at some point in the first decade of the 800s. Their younger half brother Charles was born in 823.

Lothair's first port of call was to demand oaths of loyalty from noblemen all over Francia and to threaten execution for those reluctant to do so. He succeeded in his aim and then, unsurprisingly given his actions during the reign of his father, he then set his sights on snatching the lands held by his brothers. Having feigned friendly relations with his half brother Charles in Aquitaine, Lothair made no such effort with Louis the German and laid siege to one of his strongholds, eventually forcing the garrison there to flee. There was a brief standoff between the two before the situation calmed down.

Alarmed at what he heard, Charles attempted to broker peace between Lothair and Louis, playing on the promises they had made to their father on his deathbed. But loyalty was not Lothair's strong point and, after the brief skirmishes of 840, the situation would worsen in 841 and both sides would pay a heavy price.

Characteristically, Louis the German doesn't seem to have been too different to Lothair. They and Pepin had risen against their father in unison and so it should have been no surprise to anybody that war would break out between the two. Charles, on the other hand, seems to have been the most level headed of the trio, at least in his earlier years. When civil war was beginning to look inevitable, he was the one that attempted to mediate between the other two, pledging his loyalty to Lothair if his rights and lands were acknowledged. However, that was all to no avail and he too was forced into action when direct threats were made to his mother and the pledges of loyalty he had received were proved false as key noblemen switched their allegiance to Lothair who could now see plenty of opportunity to expand his kingdom and snatch power from his brothers.

Despite successfully rescuing his mother from potential harm, Charles now found himself in trouble. Lothair had now decided to harass him and with the help of Pepin, the son of Lothair's brother of the same, surrounded Charles. Much like the scene with Louis, Lothair found himself in a standoff with Charles' men who were quite willing to fight him although Charles himself sought a peaceful resolution, something Lothair would not agree to unless he would benefit substantially. Although a temporary truce was agreed, Lothair still had designs on stealing Charles' lands and sent some of his new allies, who had crossed over from Charles' camp, into Aquitaine to wreak havoc.

Lothair's next move in 841 was to gather a large army and march on Louis who, like Charles' previously, found himself in a great dilemma and completely outnumbered. His situation was only made worse by some of his men either defecting or fleeing. The only pragmatic solution for him at this point was to retreat, which he did so, to Bavaria.

In May of 841, Charles sought yet again to reach some sort of agreement with Lothair but, showing his treacherous side again, Lothair failed to show up at the agreed meeting place. Envoys did arrive from Louis seeking an alliance with Charles against their bullying older brother. Despite last ditch attempts to prevent a battle, the inevitable finally happened and the combined forces of Charles and Louis faced off against Lothair at Fontenoy which would prove to be the bloodiest in the entire history of the Franks. After hours of vicious fighting, Lothair and his men fled and although both sides sustained heavy losses, Louis and Charles won the day.

The defeat at Fontenay may have humbled other rulers but it didn't deter Lothair and, after initially gathering his forces, or what remained of them, and pursuing Louis, he then had a change of plan and went after Charles. Although Fontenay had been a major success for Louis and Charles in purely military terms, it had very little impact on them politically and Charles only real benefit in the aftermath of the battle was a few defectors from Lothair's camp crossing over to Charles, giving a small boost to his depleted ranks. Once more Charles resorted to diplomacy and tried to reason with Lothair, urging him to adhere to the wishes of their father and the division of the kingdom. Charles must have known this was a largely futile act and there was another standoff between the two sides near Paris in late 841. This time it was Lothair who tried negotiating and offered Charles the region west of the Seine except Aquitaine. Charles was sensible enough to realise this was total folly and trusting Lothair by this point would be completely ridiculous and he rejected the offer and again referred back to what Louis the Pious had arranged for on his bed.

As he had well and truly proved, Lothair's diplomatic skills were sorely lacking and after ignoring offers from Saxony for a potential alliance in his struggle with Charles and Louis, he pushed the Saxons into the arms of his rivals and gave him a greater problem than he already had. The tide seemed to be turning against the Frankish king and he narrowly escaped the clutches of Louis and Charles when he had to make a hasty retreat from Sinzig and left Francia altogether with only a few men to escort him.

Louis and Charles headed to the capital at Aachen where now they had to have urgent discussions to resolve an escalating crisis. Lothair, rather than backing down from his aim of snatching his brothers land, had decided it better to abandon his kingdom and duty of governance altogether.

In 843, the unrest was finally put to bed with the Treaty of Verdun. Lothair continued as king of Middle Francia, and effectively made Holy Roman Emperor, Louis became king in the east while Charles ruled over the west, including overlordship of their nephew Pepin who received Aquitaine. After the agreement was reached, the three went their separate ways. Lothair to Aachen, Charles to make an advantageous marriage and Louis to his new kingdom in the East.

In 844, Lothair sought to ensure that, as Holy Roman Emperor, the right to choose the next Pope would be his and sent diplomats to the current pope to lay down the law. The discussions went well but relations between the Empire and the papacy would be a long and complicated one for centuries to come. In October of that year, Lothair, Louis and Charles met and swore loyalty to each other. The Treaty of Verdun, now that the lines of territory had been drawn, seems to have restored some brotherly affection between the

three of them.

However, the following year, 845, disaster befell Charles in his western kingdom as the Vikings sailed up the River Seine, possibly led by the semi legendary Ragnor Lothbrok, causing death and destruction on the way as they headed straight for Paris. They were appeased only after they had received a substantial pay off from Charles but, as anybody who knows even the slightest detail about Viking history could tell you, this was not a tactic that would keep them away forever.

Despite Lothair uniting with his brothers in condemning the Viking attacks on the Frankish kingdoms and threatening to wage war on them, this proved to be as useless as paying the Danes off as the men from the North were not exactly adverse to a battle. Throughout the empire, there was further trouble in Italy as Lothair's son Louis, who had been made king when he travelled to Rome for talks with the pope, found himself attacked by Muslim invaders. Lothair was obliged to send in his own forces in 848 to regain territory that the Muslims had taken. Also that same year, Lothair and Charles seem to have nearly come to blows again, perhaps the pressure of dealing with invaders from the North and East put a strain on relations, but this time managed to come to terms again without much ado.

In keeping with tradition, Lothair had his son, Louis, crowned co emperor by Pope Leo IV, which would have been a huge boost to his morale given the challenges he, his father and the empire were facing. Lothair now resorted to a similar tactic that Charles had employed against the Danish invaders and bribed them. Rather than financial though, he offered them land to settle in which, in the following century, would occur again when Normandy "land of the Norsemen" would be given to the Danes.``

With relations now good between Charles and Lothair , the one remaining family member to still be causing grief was Pepin, their nephew and Charles, after discussions with Lothair, had him sent off to a monastery. In 853, Lothair became godfather to Charles' daughter. A decade on from Verdun, the relations between these two in particular was unrecognisable. There did seem to come an element of mistrust between Louis the German and the other two, although it would simmer down.

In Autumn 855, sensing that death was coming for him, Lothair entered a monastery and took on the life of a monk for his remaining days and weeks. When he died in late September, he must have been a weary man. Aged about 60, he had seen a lot of despair and trouble in Europe, a lot of which he had caused himself. Repeated rebellions and fallings out with his father and then brothers distracted him from his duty of governing. While his father and grandfather had ruled dutifully, establishing their authority where others wished to undermine, Lothair had spent too long trying to overreach himself, acting opportunistically against Charles and Louis. However, after Verdun and becoming Emperor, he does seem to have become a better ruler, using diplomacy better. It is unfortunate for him that his time as Emperor coincided with the Viking raids becoming stronger and more devastating. As he lay dying, Lothair may have wondered if he hadn't been so quarrelsome in his early years, he could have left a lasting legacy. The Vikings put paid to that.

Louis II was the son of Lothair I, born about 825. His father, as I have already written about, had something of a controversial career, deposing his father twice, quarrelling with his brothers, eventually going to war with them before eventual reconciliation and all that, just in time to deal with the increasing threat of the Vikings to the Carolingian empire. Lothair died in 855. He had, as was becoming tradition, crowned his son Louis king of Italy in 844 and also had him crowned co Emperor in 850;

Louis' crowning as king of Italy came about when his father sent him to Italy to stamp imperial authority on the papacy but Lothair must also have had one eye on the future, given the turbulence his realm was facing at the time.. Louis, by this time, was now a young man of about 19 so extra power was only a natural move. Negotiations with Pope Sergius II were concluded successfully. Louis had established imperial control in Rome, and was now a king in his own right.

While Louis' father and uncles, Charles the Bald and Louis the German, struggled against repeated Viking raids on the Empire, Louis faced his own external threat, this time from Muslim invaders. The threat of Muslim attacks was very real in early medieval Europe, with Spain, in effect, completely conquered. Louis' kingdom in Italy came under attack in 846 with the raiders even making it as far as Rome. The danger was so real that Lothair had to intervene and sent some of his own forces into Italy where they handed the Muslims a heavy defeat. Louis then engaged them in battle himself but was defeated and narrowly escaped capture. An ignominious start for a young ruler. Were it not for his father's earlier aid, the situation could have been a lot worse for Louis.

A boost to his prestige came in 850 when Lothair sent Louis to be crowned co Emperor by Pope Leo IV. He needed it as, in 852, he sustained another blow. Attempting to regain the Muslim held Benevento, Louis was advised to pull back from the siege. While Louis procrastinated on his next move. The Muslim defenders used their unexpected respite to reinforce the city's defences. Louis had been making progress and was on the verge of making a significant gain in recapturing Benevento, when he heeded poor advice and the time and effort he and his men had put into the siege went to waste. Louis' now nearly 8 year long kingship of Italy could not be described as anything more than disappointing.

In 855, Lothair I died and Louis was now Holy Roman Emperor in his own right. He kicked things off in much the same way as his father had done by arguing with Louis the German and Charles the Bald. Like Lothair had done previously, Louis sought to siphon off some of the territory held by his uncles. Soon after, Louis then nearly came to blows with his brothers in much the same vein before diplomacy eventually won out.

Throughout Europe in the late 850s, general chaos reigned. Not only the threat of attack from Viking and Muslim invaders but also internal fighting constantly broke out, notably by Charles the Bald and Louis the German. The two had been on the same side in their dispute with Lothair but now faced off against each other. Intermittent peace talks took place but their constant squabbling thwarted any hopes of a successful, sustained and more forceful response to Viking attacks. This was a tricky time to be a ruler and Louis found out once again in 861 when his own citizens rebelled against him. It may well be they were frustrated by Louis' poor response to the Muslim invasions and perhaps the king himself was pent up with anger as he retaliated against the rebels in brutal fashion, cutting it down with "fire and sword".

In 863, Louis sought to annex Provence, much to the alarm of his brother. Talks were held and Louis seems to have come out on top as he gained Provence from the negotiations and, with his work done, went back to Italy. The following year, Louis had a disagreement with the papacy, leading to highly unsavoury scenes in Rome, where Louis' forces again demonstrated a lack of restraint against ordinary citizens. It is much to Louis' shame that this seems to have been something of a regular feature throughout his reign and the sign of a poor ruler who cannot show leniency. By this point, his reputation among contemporary chroniclers seems to be declining, one referring to him as "so called emperor". After a period of sustained violence including the raping of nuns, the rape and murder of ordinary people and the burning of churches, Louis and his men departed for Ravenna.

Towards the end of 864, Louis was seriously wounded in a hunting accident, possibly attacked by a stag. He recovered and in 866, he again launched an assault on the Muslims at Benevento, taking his wife Engelberga with him, this time proving altogether more successful. Louis's efforts looked like grounding to a halt after initial gains but in 869, he came to an agreement with the Byzantine emperor Basil I who sent him a fleet of 200 ships to give a massive boost to Louis' forces. With Benevento now captured, the entire region of Bari fell to Louis by 871.

That same year, Louis found himself on the receiving end of a plot against him after sending a rival of his wife into exile. A night attack had been planned but Louis escaped and the Beneventan rebels were brought to terms. Despite this, the man behind the plot continued to be a thorn in the side of Louis as he avoided capture himself.

In 875, Louis died aged about 50. His reign had not been an easy one. 9th century Europe was a volatile place for any ruler, capable or otherwise. Louis had shown that he was capable of strong military leadership and diplomatic skills in his recapture of Bari and his dealings with the Byzantine emperor. He had also shown a vicious, petulant streak, not a good trait in any ruler.

Charles the Bald was born in about 823. Some of his earliest memories would have been in captivity, a hostage to the machinations of his older brothers, especially Lothair and Pepin. In 830, their father, Louis the Pious, took Aquitaine off Pepin and gave it to the 7 year old Charles. This was more than enough to enrage Pepin and incite the petulant Lothair into open rebellion. They successfully deposed their father and sent him and the young boy into captivity.

For Charles, this must have been a traumatic experience and one that may well have shaped not only his world view but also the impression he had on his siblings. Certainly they would all continue to come to blows even after their father's passing in 840. Louis had outlined his plans for the boys in 817, when Lothair was crowned co Emperor, Louis the German was given the East and Pepin given lands in the south and West. The move in 830 was a miscalculation and Louis paid the price by surrendering the throne. It was only thanks to Lothair's inability to govern strongly, and on a later occasion when he deposed his father again, that saw Louis reclaim power.

Charles succeeded as king of West Francia on his father's death and almost straight away found himself fighting against Lothair who saw an opportunity to take advantage of Charles' youth and inexperience. Charles, with the support of Louis in the east, however kept Lothair in check and in 841 dealt him an almighty blow by devastating his army at the Battle of Fontenoy. Both Charles and Louis had attempted a peaceful resolution to the conflict but Lothair's headstrongedness had led to a catastrophic defeat for the now sole Emperor. The 840s continued to be a time of great upheaval for not only Charles but every European, thanks to the ever growing threat of the Viking invaders. In 845, they sacked Paris. Charles initially tried to defeat them militarily but soon had to resort to paying them off financially. This was a tactic he'd use again later in his reign to buy himself some time.

In other works on other early European kings, I have criticised this tactic of paying off Vikings as it simply only encouraged further attacks. And Charles certainly didn't stop the raids with this either. However, at least Charles did demonstrate some backbone when he claimed a victory in battle. In the aftermath of that battle, the leader of the Vikings, the king of Sweden, Bjorn Ironside, offered to pay homage to Charles. This really counted for very little as some of Bjorn's men had taken hostage one of Charles' abbots and were demanding an enormous ransom. The relations with the Vikings would continue in much the same course for the rest of the 9th century.

It wasn't only Charles' siblings that caused him a family headache but also his children. Charles had played host to the king of Wessex Athelwulf who was on his way to Rome. On his journey home, Athelwulf made arrangements to marry Charles' daughter Judith. Through this marriage, Judith became Step Mother to Alfred the Great. Judith married again after Athelwulf's death, this time to king Athelbald.

When he died not long after, she returned to her father but absconded from him and ran off with a certain Count Baldwin.

Another one of Charles' children, a son called Louis, known as the stammerer, was born in about 845. Charles had him married to a nobleman's daughter in about 856. That particular nobleman had given Charles real trouble and the marriage stabilised matters in that regard. But Louis, as he reached manhood, began to listen to ill advice and openly rebelled against his father, laying waste to the county of Anjou and attacking forces loyal to Charles. His uprising was eventually seen off and Louis eventually came back to his father. Another one of Charles' sons, also called Charles, was accidentally killed during some horse play with some companions after a day of hunting. His death is described quite graphically with a blade penetrating his brain.

Charles' queen, a woman by the name of Ermentrude, died in 869. She was well regarded by her contemporaries and also seemingly by her husband who had her involved in a number of charters. She was buried in St Denis.

Such was life in the 800s, even for royalty. Death and disaster was never far away and Charles had his fair share. The Viking threat was unquestionably the biggest threat to peace but internal disputes between Charles, Lothair and Louis the German. After 843, when the Treaty of Verdun was agreed with the clear establishment of who held what territory, relations between Charles and Lothair had improved somewhat and chroniclers even give examples of the two demonstrating brotherly affection. But having been on each other's side at Fontenoy, Charles' relationship with Louis had gone the other way and would remain troublesome throughout Charles' lifetime. When Charles, in 873, went into Italy to claim the title of Emperor, Louis, on three occasions, attempted to thwart him, putting his sons to military action. Charles saw the threats off and was crowned emperor 75 years to the day after the coronation of Charlemagne in 800, on Christmas Day 875 AD.

In late 876, Charles fell gravely ill, to the point where it was expected that he would die. He recovered enough to make long journeys throughout his kingdom but would develop another fever in 877 and this one would be fatal. A chronicler claims that he was poisoned by a Jewish doctor who he also claims Charles was extremely fond of. I think this is more likely to be nothing more than bigotry as Charles had a serious fever less than a year before his death and compromised his immune system further by his long travels.

Though his time as emperor was brief, Charles had demonstrated good qualities throughout his political career, particularly diplomatic wise. Militarily he had some considerable success, Fontenoy the most distinct and memorable. He, however, was not immune to family fall outs and his children and brothers more than a thorn in his side.

Charles the fat was born in 839, the son of Louis the German. Charles was born into a troubled world. At the time of his birth, his father was in open rebellion against the emperor, Louis the Pious (his own father). As mentioned previously, Louis the Pious had no end of problems from his sons and this time Louis the German had got wind of his father's intention to stay at Frankfurt and had promptly decided to entrench himself there with his forces and refuse his father entry. Louis senior was furious at this move but kept advancing, stopping off at Mainz where he spent Christmas. Afterwards, he attempted to negotiate with his son but Louis the German was made of stubborn stock and absolutely refused to come to terms. The emperor's next move was to retreat a little and move further down the Rhine where he managed to get some 3,000 men across the river. This gave Louis the German a tremendous problem, increased by men defecting over to the emperor, and so he fled. The emperor refused to follow him and he eventually made it to his initial

intended destination of Frankfurt.

That was the world that Charles was born into. His own father and grandfather were at complete odds with each other with regular contribution in proceedings from his uncles. His mother was a woman called Emma. Of her, there is little information but she had a comparatively long life, reaching her 70s. Women did sometimes have a role politically. For instance, Charles' aunt Ermentrude, married to Charles the Bald, was involved in royal charters but Emma does not seem to have had the same trust from her husband. She did however carry out her main function which was to produce heirs and had a number of children including three sons.

As well as the obvious threat of the Viking raids. Louis the German's kingdom in the east faced other external threats. In 853, an alliance between the Bulgar and the Slavs was reached and they attacked Louis which he managed to repulse. He had to withstand another Slavic revolt a couple of years later. All the while, Louis continued to argue with his brothers. Charles the Bald in particular didn't trust Louis as far as he could throw him. Not without some justification as Louis repeatedly threatened the borders agreed upon at Verdun in 843.

It was at this point Charles the Bald, now around 16 or 17, could start to take a more active role politically. However, the political situation was still extremely uncertain for Louis who continued to have to put down Slav rebellions and handing political power to his young son would have been a risky move. In the 860s, this was emphasised even further by the rebellion of Charles' older brother, Carloman. He made an alliance with a Slavic tribe and annexed a part of his father's kingdom. Louis responded by exiling some of Carloman's key supporters. After an extended period of disturbance. Carloman and Louis reached a peace agreement in which Louis granted to Carloman the land he had taken in exchange for a vow of loyalty.

Towards the mid 860s, Louis began to show signs of wanting to distribute more power among his sons as well as their longer term future. Charles, by now in his mid 20s, married the daughter of a count but he was left behind as his father set out on campaign against the Wends. He wanted his nephew Lothar to join him, but showing some of the treachery that is becoming quite a theme in the Carolingian family, he failed to show up for military duties. So, in his place, went Louis the younger, the middle son. Despite all that effort, the campaign ended rather dismally and Louis retreated back to Frankfurt with his tail between his legs.

In 864, Louis faced more treachery from Carloman who, after pretending to go hunting, slipped away to cause more mischief. Louis managed to make peace quicker this time. Though less seriously, Louis was left more than a little miffed when his middle son, Louis, made a marriage without his permission.

It wasn't until the 870s, that Charles the Fat began to play a more significant role in European politics. In 875, he went on behalf of his father to hold discussions with his uncle Charles the Bald, who nearly died making the effort after coming down with dysentery. That same year, the emperor Louis II died. Despite the best efforts of Louis the German, Charles the Fat and Carloman, Charles the bald had himself crowned emperor on Christmas Day 875. The response from Louis and Charles the fat was to then march into West Francia, while Charles the Bald remained in Italy, and ravaged it.

Louis the German died in 876 and the succession was divided between his three sons. By 876, Charles appeared to be in poor health as he held talks with his brother Louis the younger. Militarily, matters appeared to be taken care of by Louis and Carloman, the latter currently engaged in battle with the Wends, rather than by Charles himself. The following year it was Carloman's turn to fall ill, with it even being said he was bed bound for up to a year.

Carloman's health continued to decline and he eventually died of a stroke in 880. By this point, it seems to be Louis the Younger who was more proactive in governance. Whether he was still afflicted with his previous illness or not, Charles did make a move in 879 and took Lombardy. In 881, he joined in attacking Vienne to put down a rebellion before he secured his coronation as Emperor from Pope John VIII. Like Charles the Bald in 875, he was crowned on Christmas day.

In 882, Charles' remaining brother died. That same year, Charles decided to take up arms against the Vikings. Although not without good reason, it can only be described as that Charles bottled it and instead resorted to peace. The leader of the Viking army was baptised. In 884, became king of West Francia.

One of Charles biggest problems was that he failed to produce an heir. Was his health a factor? Possibly. He did manage to produce one child from a relationship with a mistress but his attempts to make that boy his heir failed. Through the 880s, his health went into decline again and so did his empire. Through a combination of his poor health and the ambitions of his nephew, Charles lost his grip on power in 887 and the following year, he finally died.

Charles is probably the hardest emperor to sum up really so far. In this story, there are definitely characters made of sterner stuff. Men who claimed, or attempted to claim, authority from a young age. Charles never really did that. And even as he grew older, there is a distinct lack of leadership and ruthlessness. From the late 870s, in his defence, I think his health really hindered him. For what it's worth, there is nothing to suggest he was fat and that nickname only comes much later on, so his health is unlikely to be anything caused by his size. Ultimately, he is probably the one of the most unremarkable of the 9th century emperors.

We're now coming up to a tricky part of the story. For simplicity's sake, I could skip ahead to the life and times of Otto the Great. It's questionable whether the subjects here can really be considered Holy Roman Emperors. I have decided to include them, however, for continuity's sake.

Charles the Fat's health had begun to decline through the 880s and in 887, his nephew, Arnulf of Carinthia deposed him. Whilst the move was hardly an act of affection towards his uncle, Arnulf did allow Charles to live out the rest of his days on some imperial lands left to him. This however did not mean Arnulf automatically assumed total power. He succeeded as king of East Francia but did not become emperor immediately as may have been expected.In fact, the men who had come over to Arnulf when he decided to move against the ailing emperor, deserted him. Whilst it may have seemed natural to elect Arnulf as emperor, that did not happen and the other different regions of the empire decided to elect their own rulers. In Italy, there was contention as two separate kings were declared, Berengar and Guy of Spoleto. As always with contested crowns, this inevitably led to trouble. After a period of bloodshed, Guy eventually won out and Berengar was driven from Italy. Guy became king of Italy in 889.

In West Francia, the citizens there elected a man by the name of Odo as their king. He was, by all accounts, a formidable man and he would rule over them for a decade. His election was made official after Arnulf was informed and he duly gave his consent. As can be expected, Odo's reign was largely taken up by dealing with the Vikings which he is said to have done "manfully". His successor in West Francia would be Charles the Simple who would be altogether different in his dealings with the invasions.

In 896, Arnulf marched into Italy which would see him crowned emperor. The ruler in Italy at that time was Lambert, son of Guy of Spoleto. Lambert had been crowned king of Italy when his father was made emperor in 891. Guy and Pope Formosus were not on good terms but Guy did manage to get the pope to crown Lambert co emperor in 892. Guy's actual power was extremely limited and he died in 894 with Lambert now left to try and fend off Arnulf and his machinations by himself.

After clinging onto power in Italy, Lambert made a poor decision. Whilst away from Rome, he had left his own mother to guard the city with a sizable force. Her and her army appeared not to put up a particularly stiff resistance as Arnulf marched into Italy and onto Rome. It was there that he was crowned by Pope Formosus. However, after his apparent triumph, Arnulf came down with a serious illness which, according to the chronicles at the time, was said to have gripped him for a long time. It's been suggested that he had a stroke.

After that stroke, Arnulf's health continued to get worse and he is believed to have suffered from some highly unpleasant illnesses. He eventually died in 899. Because of Arnulf's ill health, Lambert had managed to retain power but not for long. After dealing with a rebellion against him, which had been led by the same Berengar who had been defeated by Lambert's father Guy over a decade prior, Lambert was assassinated.

It's hard to judge what the legacy of these men actually was. Certainly Guy of Spoleto accomplished little. Arnulf seems militarily capable but his path to power had been borne through treachery towards his own uncle and he had died before he could fully establish a lasting legacy. As for Lambert, he too had his moments militarily but, like Arnulf, his life ended prematurely, possibly when he wasn't even out of his teens. It is largely due to factors such as these that the Emperors in this particular period have largely been forgotten.

Louis the Blind was born in about 880. He was the son of a man named Boso and his mother was a woman by the name of Ermengarde who was the daughter of the Holy Roman Emperor Louis II. In 879, Boso set out to take Provence after the death of Louis the Stammerer. Louis had left two sons whose claims Boso treated with utmost contempt while he resorted to a combination of persuasion and bullying to get influential men to support his claims to power in Provence. However he wasn't successful in winning everybody over to his cause and the two heirs to Louis the Stammerer, another Louis and Carloman, were raised to kingship to counter Boso's claims.

As such, Boso's time as King of Provence was dominated by warring against Louis and Carloman and in 882, he essentially lost most of his territory after being besieged at Vienne by his own brother. Boso was not a popular man. He was viewed as a usurper, which is exactly what he was, and treated with hostility, not only in his own realm, but by other Frankish rulers. One chronicler even implies that the other kings made their vassals swear that they would try and eliminate Boso.

Such was Boso's popularity at the time of his death in 887. While all that had been going on, his son Louis had been born in 880. The timing seems to have been quite opportune for Boso as he had only seized power the year prior and so perhaps hoped that the birth of an heir might stabilise matters for him which, for him, was unfortunately not the case. Like a lot of other children born into power in 9th century Europe, Louis came into a world dominated by infighting and corruption.

On the death of his father, when he was aged about 7, Louis and his mother moved to ensure they stayed in power and visited Charles the Fat to establish their claims over the kingdom of Provence. The emperor, who was by now in poor health, recognised Louis as king of Provence and adopted him. However, not long after, Charles was deposed by Arnulf of Carinthia and Louis had to reestablish power for himself, which he managed to do in the early 890s, before he paid homage to Arnulf of Carinthia.

In the early 900s, as Louis began to reach an age of maturity, and, in keeping with this, his power and influence grew. In Italy, there was a growing restlessness with how the country was being ruled by Berengar. And so the nobles invited Louis to take over and he was promptly crowned Emperor in 901. It wasn't to last however and Berengar reclaimed power the following year and brought Louis to terms. A couple of years later, Louis went back on the peace agreement and this is where he earned the nickname "the blind". Berengar, mimicking something usually seen in the Eastern Roman Empire, rather than totally eliminating Louis, instead had him blinded in cruel fashion.

This spelled the end of Louis' brief period as emperor but he would remain king of Provence for another 23 years. Louis kept his travels to an absolute minimum, residing in his capital for the majority of the remainder of his reign. He seems to have been a quite popular ruler with one chronicler continuing to call him "most glorious of emperors", despite his having relinquished that title long ago.

Berengar's career is one of a man used to confrontation. He had an intense rivalry with Guy of Spoleto and then saw off the challenge of Louis the Blind, initially by peace then when Louis came to challenge his rule in Italy, Berengar took the brutal step of having Louis blinded. Louis had been invited twice to invade Italy due to Berengar's unpopular rule. Born in about 845, Berengar was the grandson of Louis the Pious on his mother's side and so was the great grandson of Charlemagne. Such a prestigious family background should have been highly advantageous for Berengar.

Berengar's first taste of power came when he succeeded his older brother as Margrave of Fruili, a territory in Italy. That came about when he was aged about 19. In 875, Berengar was used by Louis the German in his desperate attempts to stop Charles the Bald from becoming Holy Roman Emperor. This was unsuccessful as Charles' saw off three attempts by Louis to thwart him but it does show Berengar's growing importance in the empire. In the mid 880's, Berengar's rivalry with Guy of Spoleto began as Charles the Fat sent him to take Spoleto off Guy. After initial success for Berengar, he and his army were driven back by a plague.

In 887, Berengar managed to lose the favour of Charles the Fat after he got himself entangled in a dispute with a powerful bishop. Berengar went back to the emperor in grovelling fashion and managed to get himself back in the good books of Charles. At this point, Berengar must have been fully aware of the political situation in the empire as Charles was deprived of power that year and so by placing himself close at hand, he put himself in a position to extend his power and he became king of Italy.

However, not long after his succession to power, Berengar's nemesis Guy of Spoleto was back on the scene and challenging Berengar's rule. They came to blows near Brescia where the result was inconclusive and a peace treaty was agreed upon although only lasted for a matter of months. Berengar then had to see off Arnulf of Carinthia which he did so but Arnulf effectively became Berengar's overlord.

Berengar's authority was then thoroughly undermined by Guy who defeated him at Trebbia and had himself declared king of Italy. This was shortly after the initial peace treaty had expired. After a brief pause in hostilities, 893/894 saw Berengar unite with Arnulf in an attempt to deprive Guy of power. They initially defeated Guy and gained territory before a combination of Guy fighting back and Berengar and Arnulf having a major disagreement saw Berengar lose Fruili and temporarily driven from Italy. Guy, however, died that year and the rivalry with Berengar passed on from him to his son Lambert.

Berengar challenged Lambert's rule in Italy but was defeated in battle. Lambert, however, was murdered at the age of just 18 and this left Berengar's path back to power clear. In 899, though, his rule suffered a severe blow when he was routed by the invading Magyars'. This prompted the nobility to seriously question Berengar and it was here that Louis, king of Provence, was invited to invade Italy and usurp Berengar. The next few years were blighted by Louis and Berengar's feuding and the Magyars repeated attacks. Berengar saw off the threat of Louis by capturing and blinding him.

Magyar invasions were not the only threat to the empire at this time. Saracen invasions had been an almost constant thorn in the side of the rulers of Italy and in 915, the high point of Berengar's political career came to fruition with the defeat of the Muslim invaders at Garigliano. This prompted the pope to crown Berengar Holy Roman Emperor.

His reign as emperor was completely overshadowed by continued problems. The Magyars continued to sack and loot and in 923 Berengar faced another challenge to his status as emperor when he was faced off in battle by the king of Burgundy and his allies. The battle proved to be a total disaster for Berengar who was roundly defeated and effectively saw him removed from power. Not long after, he was murdered.

A man of considerable family pedigree, Berengar was clearly not the shrewdest or most able of rulers. Frequently defeated in battle and a man who regularly lost territory he held, he also had a nasty streak as shown by his treatment of Louis the Blind. His stand out achievement was clearly the events of 915 but unfortunately for Berengar and those he ruled over, he failed to put it to much use and his lack of military prowess ensured that his time as emperor was blighted by further Magyar raids and civil war.

Otto I was the son of Henry The Fowler, who himself was king of Germany between 919 and 936. Henry's early career was dominated by a marriage controversy. His attention had been caught by a woman called Hatheburg. She was a widow who'd sworn to take the veil after the death of her first husband. However, this didn't put off Henry who was extremely eager to marry her and indeed the wedding did take place. Among the clergy, though, there was extreme disquiet over the match. Henry, not wishing to give in, went to seek the advice of the German king at the time, Conrad I. Conrad seemed to sympathise with Henry and attempted to mediate between Henry and the clergy. In the end, though, Henry and Hatheburg's marriage was dissolved. In 909, Henry made a second marriage. This time his bride was a woman by the name of Matilda. She was the daughter of a Saxon nobleman and would prove to be the mother of Henry's heir, Otto.

Conrad I died in late 918. Before he died, he advised his nobility that they should elect Henry as his heir. He did this despite there being a breakdown in relations between himself and Henry through the 910s. Conrad's options were really limited as he had no children as his heirs so, looking to the future, he had to put aside any ill will he might have had towards Henry in order to avoid civil war in his kingdom. The nobility agreed to elect Henry king and he was crowned about 6 months after the death of Conrad.

The chroniclers are generous in their praise of Henry. Widukind calls him " the father of his country and the greatest and best of all kings". Thietmar of Merseburg shares in those sentiments and says that the qualities that can be seen in Henry could also be found in his son Otto. Things didn't necessarily get off to the easiest start for Henry however. On coming to the throne, he insisted on certain regions, including Bohemia, on paying tribute to him. This didn't go down well and the territories in question responded by rebelling against Henry. After a period, Henry managed to bring the Bohemians back into line.

But a far bigger problem then came in the shape of the Magyar invasions. This had been a constant problem in Europe since the previous century and Henry had to find a way of dealing with this threat. Initially, he attempted to react by force but he came unstuck and was defeated in battle. His next tactic was essentially to agree to a peace treaty and pay them off. Bribing invading forces would not last forever however and, indeed, the Magyars would continue to be a thorn in the side for Henry for most of his reign.

Henry would strengthen his realm by building defensive fortifications and bringing rebellious regions back under control. He had successes against the Vikings, no mean feat in itself, and helped to Christianise some of his pagan enemies. Widukind speaks of Henry's growing stature and confidence as he continues to put down challenges to his authority.

Henry had repeated struggles against the king of West Francia, Charles the Simple who ended his career in captivity. Pretending to be saddened by this, Henry hoped to take another of Charles' possessions, Lotharangia, which he first intended to do by diplomacy if he could help it. The region, after Charles' death, had technically become the property of a man named Gislebert. Having met Gislebert and seeing first hand a young man of noble birth with the qualities required to rule, Henry reconsidered the matter and had Gislebert marry his daughter. This was a canny move. To all intents and purposes, Lotharangia was still in his hands and had at the same time also made his a daughter a good marriage.

The next item on the agenda for Henry was to secure his dynasty and produce heirs. After the dissolution of his first marriage, he married Matilda. This marriage was successful in its primary purposes in that it provided Henry with sons and heirs. Two of them would becomes Dukes of Bavaria and Lotharangia respectively. The first born, Otto, would become one of the most renowned of all early medieval European rulers.

Queen Matilda also had something of an interesting family history. Some of her distant relations had been involved in the Saxon wars that would plague Charlemagne over a century earlier and her uncles had fought against the Vikings. The fact her son became known as Otto the Great firmly establishes her place in history.

During the nine year peace treaty with the Magyars, Henry had not only been on a programme of fortress building but also had put in place plans for the men he had to garrison them. They were to train day and night in preparation for any invasion that might come and he planned extensively to ensure that the men had the required provisions. These new strongholds would also be used for law courts and assemblies. These forts were especially needed. Widukind tells of the sparse strongholds throughout the kingdom that were either poorly maintained or damaged from repeated civil wars or from battles and sieges against the Magyars and other peoples.

Thoughts now turned to Otto and his future. A match was made for him with Eadgyth, the daughter of King Edward the Elder. According to Widukind, she was popular with the people and would produce for Otto two children, a son and a daughter. The marriage came at a particularly successful time for Henry in his campaigns against the Magyars. He had secured the succession, Otto would succeed him as ruler of all his territories on his death in 936, repulsed Viking incursions and ruled over his kingdom with shrewdness and authority. When he died aged around 60, his citizens mourned his passing. Widukind calls him the best of Europe's kings. He left his son an extended kingdom to rule over. Henry's most enduring legacy though would prove to be Otto.

Otto I became king of Germany in 936 on the death of his father. Henry the Fowler had left a kingdom in strong health for Otto. After the nobles had sworn to uphold Henry's wishes that Otto would succeed him, the coronation for Otto to become king of Germany took place at Aachen in 936. An argument arose at the ceremony over who would oversee the proceedings before it was settled upon a senior Archbishop by the name of Hildibert. After Hildibert made Otto swear the usual oaths of ruling justly and upholding peace, they anointed him as king. When the coronation was completed, the royal party headed to the palace for celebratory feasts.

One of Otto's main problems, as had been the case during his father's reign, was dealing with the Magyars. In 955, they had sent ambassadors to Otto's court in the pretence of seeking peace but it was merely a trick. Once the ambassadors had left with gifts from the king, Magyar forces spilled into the German kingdom, causing carnage. Otto reacted immediately, where he would meet them at the battle of Lechfeld.

The battle, to begin with, didn't go as planned. The Magyars crossed the river Lech and caught Otto's forces off guard. Significant damage was caused to the rear of Otto's army as many men were either killed or taken captive. Otto, with the help of his Dukes, managed to reorganise and reclaimed most of the men who had been taken by the Magyars and put to flight the initial attack. Otto now sensed blood as the Magyars retreated and launched his own counter attack against them, sending them into disarray. The enemy fled in panic, some drowning, some being hunted down by Otto's men and being brutally burned alive in nearby buildings in the neighbouring town. Widukind describes the victory as there "never being so bloody a victory gained over so savage a people". He also describes there being virtually no survivors on the Magyar side. The victory was absolute.

This brilliant military victory at Lechfeld typifies the type of man Otto was. Much of what Otto learned would have been gleaned from his father's own brilliant military victories against the Magyars and Danes. Otto was born in about 912 so would have been in his early twenties when he became German king. His added maturity at the time of his coronation would certainly stand him in good stead.

Otto's realm had been disturbed by the actions of a certain Boleslav I who murdered one of Henry The Fowler's allies. The problems with Boleslav continued into the 940s, before Otto eventually captured him and placed him in the custody of Duke Henry of Bavaria, one of Otto's brothers.

In 930, Otto married his first wife, Eadgyth, the daughter of Edward the Elder of Wessex and so granddaughter of Alfred the Great. She produced him a son and daughter and proved to be popular both with the ordinary people and with Otto. She died aged about 35 and Otto grieved her passing. Otto's second wife was a woman by the name of Adelaide who would yield much influence and will be mentioned in greater detail in part three of this blog on Otto the great and also in the following reign of Otto II, her son with Otto I.

Ruling over an extensive territory involved considerable travelling for any diligent king and it was during one of these journeys that Otto unearthed a plot against him, formulated by his son Liudolf and by one of his other male relations by marriage although there is some confusion as to who was the guilty party; either his brother in law Hugh or son in law Conrad. Either way, the man responsible had clearly been whispering in Liudolf's ear as Otto had been quite clear in his intentions to share power with his son. The rebellion became serious with Bavaria in particular turning their backs on Otto. Disgusted by this, he ransacked the neighbouring countryside, leaving the citizens in no doubt as to his feelings towards them. Liudolf had also attempted to capture Mainz. One of the key men in the uprising then made matters worse in 954 by allying himself with the Magyars, just a year before Lechfeld. After causing a substantial amount of damage to the king's forces, the rebels then incited Otto to go back to Bavaria and besiege that region again after their previous treachery.

The rebellion eventually petered out with Liudolf and his allies eventually realising they had no hope of winning though this wouldn't stop Liudolf from uprising again shortly before his death in 957. Despite all the troubles his son had caused him, Otto was deeply upset when news of Liudolf's passing had been brought to him.

After a civil war against his own son and wars against the Magyars, Otto took a break from defensive wars and invaded Lombardy in 961 where he removed the troublesome king of Italy Berengar II from power and sent him into exile. The next step for Otto on his road to greatness now was to have himself crowned Holy Roman Emperor which he would achieve the following year.

After his exploits in Lombardy, Otto headed to Rome where he would spend Christmas 961. It was in early February 962 that Otto was crowned Holy Roman Emperor by Pope John XII. Even though Berengar had formally been deposed by Otto, he was still deemed a sufficient enough threat to peace in the empire that the imperial army turned their attentions back towards him where he was besieged at San Leo. There was an unsettling turn of events for Otto as the Pope who had crowned him Emperor decided to ally himself with Berengar's son. This could be considered surprising as Berengar had previously invaded papal held territory.

When they heard that Otto was once more on his way to Rome, Pope John and Berengar's son, named Adalbert, didn't waste any time in fleeing the city, carrying with them as many riches as they could possibly manage.Support in Rome was divided. Some sympathised with John, others sided with the Emperor. However, whatever the general feeling was, the city paid due respect to Otto when he arrived. Once there, Otto held a synod with leading bishops to decide what to do with the now absent Pope. It was decided that John should be restored to power but once he refused the request for his return, he was deposed and elected in his stead was Pope Leo VIII.

In 967, Otto had his son, also called Otto, crowned co emperor. The elder Otto then sought a marriage alliance for his son and with that he turned to the Byzantine empire. The relations between east and west were not always easy and so it proved again in these negotiations. On their way to the Byzantine court, some members of Otto's embassy were set upon and killed. Needless to say Otto wasn't impressed and reacted in kind. The situation settled enough that a Byzantine empress, by the name of Theophanu, was sent to the west where she'd marry the future Otto II.

Theophanu was the niece of the Byzantine emperor John I and would go on to forge an excellent reputation for herself, rising to co empress and acting as regent too. More on her later during my next blog on Otto II. Another key woman during these years was Otto I's second wife Adelaide. Her name appears frequently in her husband's charters and it was through her that, after he had deposed Berengar, Otto could now claim to be king of Italy.

Between them, Otto and Adelaide had effectively unified the Holy Roman Empire. Adelaide would continue to be an important figure even after Otto I's death and will be mentioned again when we reach the reign of their son Otto II.

Otto I's relations with the papacy would continue to be difficult and Pope Leo VIII had now also been deposed, this time by the people of Rome. John XII returned briefly before dying and Benedict V was his replacement. However, Otto asserted his imperial authority and made the Romans reinstate Leo as pope. There would be further problems with the papacy throughout the 960s.

Otto I spent the last 10 months of his life back in Germany, having finally left Italy in 972. He had, with not little difficulty, established imperial authority over Italy, having brought it into the empire with his marriage to Adelaide, improved, again with no shortage of issues, relations with the Byzantine empire by marrying his son off to a Byzantine princess and left the succession secure with his son crowned co emperor. Through strong resolve, he became Otto The Great.

Born in 955, the son of Otto the Great, Otto had some act to follow. His father is regarded as the first true Holy Roman Emperor since Charlemagne. His life would be altogether brief, however, dying at the age of just 28. His short career included being crowned emperor alongside his father in 967 when he was still only 11 and marrying a Byzantine princess.

When Otto I died in 973, his now 18 year old son again went through the formalities of being anointed king, even though he had done so on being crowned co emperor in 967. His childhood seems to have been normal and Thietmar describes him as being a happy and fortunate child. Otto is also described as being physically imposing with a tendency to become reckless. As a young man, he showed signs of being overly proud and slightly headstrong but would outgrow many of these early failings and learned to listen to those around with more worldly experience. He was a pious man and was generous towards the clergy. He offered the monks at Magdeburg a book containing portraits of himself and his queen, Theophanu.

Otto had married Theophanu in 972, a year before he became sole emperor. With him, she seems to have enjoyed a good relationship, joining him on his travels and being raised to the status of co empress. There were some chroniclers who were somewhat sniffy towards her. Perhaps because she was Byzantine or perhaps because, as a woman, she was no shrinking violet. Another strong female figure in the life of Otto II was Adelaide, his mother, who outlived both Otto and Theophanu and is said to have been quite glad when Theophanu died in 991. When she became regent on behalf of her and Otto's son, Theophanu seems to have governed sensibly enough.

Thietmar describes Otto's continued generosity towards the church, including Thietmar's own place of residence at Merseburg, granting the Bishops their lands and abbeys for their own benefit. Otto faced some problems in his realm with a rebellion being led by Duke Henry II of Bavaria. Having initially captured him and placed him in prison, Otto may have thought he had brought the trouble to a halt. Thietmar does describe the prison as being secure and well guarded. This couldn't have been the case however and Duke Henry escaped, proclaiming himself emperor. This time Otto threw his full force at the Duke; deposed, excommunicated and besieged, Henry was forced to flee for his life and didn't regain his duchy until over a decade after Otto's death.

While the troubles with Duke Henry were ongoing, Otto had shown his potential as a military leader. First, he captured a defensive fortification held by two troublesome brothers in what was Otto's first campaign. He then followed that up by clashing with the Danes. Whilst the enemy seemed to be set up to thwart him, Otto managed to overpower them. To protect his kingdom from any further incursions from Harald Bluetooth and his men, Otto set up defensive structures at Schleswig where the Danes had intruded.

Otto then found himself embroiled in a war against the king of France, Lothair, with Lothair launching an assault against the Emperor at the imperial capital at Aachen. Taking up arms, Otto declared war on the French king. Having caused considerable damage at Aachen, Lothair then beat a hasty retreat with Otto now in hot pursuit. Otto returned in kind the damage caused by Lothair by laying France to waste all the way up to Paris. He then besieged Paris where illness and disease seems to have set in among the defenders. Having firmly made his point, Otto withdrew.

In 980, relations between Otto and Lothair seem to have been mended with Lothair appearing before the emperor, loaded with gifts. Like his father, Otto had proved himself to be a strong leader in times of trouble and this show of homage from Lothair must have been gratifying for him. It was in that same year that Otto's son and heir, also called Otto, was born. The baby was born shortly before the emperor left for Italy where he would spend the remainder of his reign.

Throughout his reign, whether the threat came from Frank, Dane or Saracen, Otto kept an iron fist grip on his territory and responded to any invasion with brute force, driving back the enemy from whence they came. In Calabria, the emperor had to deal with the nuisance that was the Byzantine empire as the east and west's turbulent relationship continued. And at Talanto, Otto regained the captured city from the

Byzantines. Such was Otto's wide spread accomplishments. From thwarting Lothair, to halting the machinations of the Eastern Roman Empire in the south of his kingdom, Otto had shown potential for greatness in his own right. What tarnished his reputation in the eyes of history, however, is the simple fact he died far too young. His heir was a mere toddler and with child rulers comes anarchy. The strong rule of the first two Ottos was about to come undone.

Otto III became king of Germany in late 983. He had spent his years as an infant in Italy where Otto II had been putting out fires with invasions coming from the Saracens and the Byzantine empire. Other problems had occurred during Otto II's reign and one of the biggest issues was the troublesome Duke of Bavaria Henry II known, quite appropriately, as "the quarrelsome". After rebelling twice against Otto II, on the second occasion declaring himself emperor, Henry had been emphatically defeated and put into secure custody (After his first rebellion had ended in failure, Henry had likewise been imprisoned but through hook or by crook, he had escaped).

Showing no signs of feeling chastised by his failures, Henry had been released from his captivity on the death of Otto II. He was a cousin of Otto III and so, by right, this made him lawful guardian of the young boy. And so here, being a man who could sense an opportunity, Henry would have realised that with a child king effectively under his command, he had a very real chance of becoming sole king. He gathered a group of powerful nobles around him and asked for their backing as he attempted to snatch power. The nobles were reluctant to do so, however, and their meeting ended in serious tension with some excusing themselves from support, perhaps fearing another civil war, while others, sensing Henry's growing irritation at the lack of enthusiasm for his plot, withdrew from the meeting altogether. Whilst he did have some supporters, Henry had managed to alienate key figures who remained loyal to the little Otto and now swore to thwart any further attempt from Henry to claim the crown.

Around Easter of 984, Henry's support continued to grow with three dukes called Miesco, Mistui and Boleslaw, among others, all swearing loyalty to him as their king. However, there were also now plots against Henry that were quite out in the open, causing him no little alarm. He responded by winning over members of the clergy in Bohemia but ultimately Henry began to see that the situation was escalating beyond his control and, in the summer of 985, finally put an end to his bid for the crown by handing over Otto back to his mother, Theophanu, who now became regent. Whilst there is little good to say about Henry The Quarrelsome, he at the very least kept his young cousin alive. With such grand plans for power as he had, Henry might have "done away with" Otto, in the fashion of other more ruthless figures throughout medieval history. It must have been a tremendous relief for Theophanu to be reunited with her son. His fate, during his two year absence, would have been quite unknown to her.

The following Easter, in 986, matters continued to stabilise with followers of Henry coming to Otto's court and bestowing gifts upon him. One of those gifts, given to the king by Duke Miesco, was a camel which may well have bemused the 6 year old. The next five years of Otto's life were relatively peaceful (or as peaceful as you could get in 10th century Europe). That was in part down to the capable rule of his mother. A blow was to befall the eleven year old Otto, though, when, in 991, Theophanu died. His grandmother Adelaide succeeded as regent. Given the fact that Adelaide was not particularly sorry at the death of Theophanu, it's probably fair to say, as he reached his mid teens, that Otto would have been relieved to relinquish her of power and become ruler in his own right.

Like his father, Otto was traditionally pious and made great effort to maintain the welfare of the church. In 995, Otto held a meeting in order to settle a dispute between Henry The Quarrelsome and one of his rivals. Through a combination of good counsel from the king and Henry perhaps sensing he didn't have long left, the matter was settled without too much ado. Henry died not long after with words of sage advice to his own son. Henry ordered him not to rebel against his king and overlord and demanded he maintained peace in Bavaria and governed justly. And in late August, he died, ending a memorable career.

In the winter of that same year, Otto defeated the Slavs in battle in what were very unforgiving conditions. The initial Slavic attack had been a strong one with the king's army scattering before it. Laying siege to key defensive structures, the Slavs could have caused serious harm had Otto not eventually dispersed them with everything he had at his disposal. The threat to peace had been caused by a man named Kizo who had gone over to the Slavs. Otto treated him with leniency, by restoring Kizo to the territories he had initially been deprived of. Not that it benefited him much as Kizo was killed soon after. This had still been a feather in the cap of Otto. He had, despite only being 15, demonstrated that he was reaching manhood by a combination of military leadership and managing problematic men of influence.

The following year, Otto headed into Italy where he would be made Holy Roman Emperor. From there, Otto's travels were far and wide. He stabilised matters in Italy, visited Romania before dealing with another uprising by the Slavs in 997. He also headed back to Germany, ensuring peace in his kingdom. A crisis arose in Rome when, whilst the rightful pope was away, a usurper had been put in his place. Then, to make matters worse, the messengers that had been sent to Rome by Otto were captured and effectively taken hostage. Otto was thus obliged to march on Rome and restore order. The usurper, John of Calabria, unsurprisingly panicked when he heard the imperial army was heading towards him and so fled. He didn't escape long though and paid the price by having his eyes, nose and tongue cut off.

Otto, in the year 1000, visited Aachen and the resting place of Charlemagne. Rather tactlessly, and what must have caused some deal of disapproval, he opened the tomb of Charles The Great and removed relics and hung them from his own neck. This is a strong indicator of how he wished to see himself in history and he perhaps might have achieved similar greatness were it not for his premature death in 1002, aged just 21.

The cause of his death was unclear and came at a very inopportune time. He was a young man just finding his feet as emperor and was just about to, as his father had done, marry a Byzantine princess. She was Zoe, daughter of Constantine VIII, and would be empress too. This now meant he died without siring an heir and securing the succession. This would have serious consequences.

Henry II was born in Bavaria in 973. His father was Henry The Quarrelsome. As you can probably deduce from his nickname, Henry The Quarrelsome was a disruptive figure in European politics, leading revolts and plotting to seize power and become Holy Roman Emperor. He had attempted to usurp his infant cousin Otto III and gained some strong support for it but the young boy's following was ultimately more loyal and stood firmly by the young German king and future emperor.

As a character, Henry seems to have been altogether more amenable then his father who, on his deathbed in August 995, gave him strict instruction to not behave in the manner that he had done and to govern wisely. After he had concluded, he ordered Henry to head back to Bavaria and become Duke. The son left without hesitation. It may have affected him deeply to leave his father dying on his deathbed but, like an obliging son should, he heeded his father's instructions.

In 999, Henry finally got married, to a woman named Cunigunde. His nobility may have thought it was not before time too. Henry was now in his mid twenties and would need to think about his succession. On this score, the marriage was a failure as it produced no children and the match would only benefit Henry in the sense that it extended his sphere of influence. Ironically though, Henry himself would benefit from another ruler also not producing heirs. In 1002, the Holy Roman

Emperor Otto III died aged 21 and without issue. This caused the empire a major problem.

Rebellions were a common theme in early medieval Europe and Otto III, the year before he died, asked Henry, as duke of Bavaria, to assist him in putting down trouble in Italy. The issue had been a plot to kidnap Otto III. The culprit was a man by the name of Gregory who, according to Thietmar of Merseburg, was held in high regard by Otto and had, up to that point at least, been a stalwart supporter of the emperor. Otto escaped that plot but died the following year in 1002. There are questions over the circumstances of his death. Was it murder? Otto was only 21 and Thietmar tells of schemes and plots aplenty against the life of Otto from various, would be usurpers. There is no hard evidence of that but his death can certainly be put in the suspicious category.

During the plots against Otto, there had been some who wished to gain the help of Duke Henry in deposing the emperor but Henry refused, stating his loyalty to the emperor. But with the emperor now dead, Henry made his move and did so at the funeral. Thietmar tells of Henry trying to gain the support of the nobility to have himself crowned king of Germany. But he didn't have much luck in that regard and so headed back to Germany, escorting the body of the former emperor.

There, a rival claimant was set up against Henry, with a certain Duke Herman gaining support from the nobility. As had happened before, on the death of an emperor, the empire faced divisions. Not only in Germany but elsewhere too. In Lombardy, they had their own king crowned, a man by the name of Arduin. But Henry did gain the support of the Saxons and so made his move to be crowned king of Germany. It would not go uncontested and his support was as far from universal as you could possibly get,

Henry, as a young man, is described as being conventionally pious and a brilliant pupil. He would need some of that brilliance simply to hold on to power. The aforementioned Herman, Duke of Swabia proved to be his biggest rival. By marriage, Herman was related to Otto The Great and this, he believed, trumped any claim Henry had. The dispute rumbled deep into 1002, when Henry, after a serious struggle, finally defeated his rival. Perhaps wishing to avoid civil war, Herman submitted with Henry allowing him to keep Swabia. The following year though, Henry effectively pinched the Duchy when Herman died, leaving a young son as his heir. Henry didn't relinquish control and added it to his expanding territory. Through a combination of stubborn military action, diplomacy and a little luck, Henry's power was now growing.

Established as king of Germany, Henry now set his eyes further afield into Italy and beyond.

After he finally subdued the rebellion of Duke Herman of Swabia, Henry continued to consolidate power as German king. In August of 1002, his wife Cunigunde was crowned queen. He processed through the kingdom, trying to gain as much support as he could. After a delay with the Lotharingians, he eventually had oaths sworn to him by the bishops there who proceeded to accompany him to Aachen. At Aachen, the leading members of the Lotharingian nobility also joined in declaring their approval of Henry as their king. His prestige and authority was slowly growing.

As I mentioned in part one, the men of Lombardy, on the death of Otto III, had decided to elect their own king, a man by the name of Arduin. This was something they came to regret fairly swiftly. Arduin, on hearing the grown strength of Henry in Germany, had taken steps to secure his own position. He strengthened defensive fortifications and garrisoned them. But he also disillusioned his clergy. In one instance, he threw a bishop to the ground by his hair in a fit of petulant rage after the bishop had said things Arduin simply didn't want to hear. After matters such as these, the bishops of Lombardy asked for assistance from King Henry.

The initial response to Arduin's mischief was not successful. The Germans sent into Italy were faced off by a headstrong Arduin and, in one of their first encounters, it was he who came out on top although not without losses on his side. The Germans had been thrown off somewhat by the desertion of one of their dukes. While that was going on in Italy, Henry continued to process through Germany, attempting to administer law and order where and when he could and seems to be relatively successful.

In 1003, Henry received some grim news from Bohemia and Poland regarding two dukes by the name of Boleslaw. Boleslaw of Bohemia had acted unscrupulously and murdered his own brother in law as well as a number of important noblemen. Boleslaw of Poland had got wind of this. Not particularly sorry at what had happened, he summoned his counterpart to Poland where he had him blinded and exiled. Boleslaw of Poland then made his way swiftly to Prague where he had himself made lord. He had used the crisis entirely to his benefit. This potentially gave King Henry a problem. Boleslaw had not only shown himself to be a ruthless man of action but also one who was now growing over-mighty.and this simply wouldn't do. He demanded homage from Boleslaw who disregarded it. For a short time, Henry let the situation rest but it wasn't long before Boleslaw was in open rebellion.

Through the remainder of 1003, Henry focused his attention on one of Boleslaw's key allies, Margrave Henry. The rivalry between Margrave Henry and king Henry was personal as their fathers had also clashed . King Henry, however, soon got on top, dealing him a serious blow by besieging one of the margrave's burgs and killing a number of his men. Meanwhile, Boleslaw continued to plot and conspire against the king and lay waste to regions held by men loyal to Henry. The margrave now sensed that Boleslaw was his best hope of success and so went to join him. Before he departed his burg, he burned it to the ground, perhaps hoping to ensure that the king wouldn't benefit from it. Henry was pleased when he saw this. He was tracking the margrave's progress slowly and so must have deduced that his enemy was running out of options.

Into 1004 and there were tit for tat clashes. Boleslaw attacked Bavaria so Henry attacked one of his territories. There was finally some respite for the king as the margrave finally gave in and came grovelling for forgiveness. Henry had him imprisoned and turned his attentions back towards Italy. When Arduin heard of the king's arrival, he became instantly terrified and once again reinforced the defences of Lombardy. However, Arduin, by now, had alienated enough of his subjects that progress for Henry was not difficult and in May 1004, he was crowned king of Italy

Henry, straight away however, was faced by another rebellion. Evidently, Arduin had done something right and an uprising to reinstall him to power took place with an attack being launched on the king's palace. Henry was eventually successful in calming the situation and, after securing the loyalty of the chastised rebels, continued to progress through Lombardy.

Unlike some of his predecessors, Henry didn't linger in Italy too long and made his way swiftly back to Germany. That was more than likely due to his concern about Boleslaw who continued to be a thorn in his side. Taking the attack to Boleslaw in 1005, Henry marched into Poland but paid a heavy price. To buy himself some time, he eventually managed to come to a peace agreement with Boleslaw. But Henry must have known that wouldn't be honoured for very long and it was he himself who reneged on the treaty. Further periods of fighting and then peace broke out before a marriage agreement was made as Boleslaw's son married a granddaughter of Otto II. Boleslaw is known to history as "The Brave" and he certainly showed that he was a man not shy of a fight. Even after Henry's succession as emperor in 1014, relations between the two continued in much the same vein. .

In 1014, Henry's problems were much the same as they had been earlier in his reign. Arduin continued to cause problems for him in Italy and Boleslaw the Brave hadn't gone away either. Henry had initially driven Arduin out of Lombardy in 1004 and took advantage of this by having himself crowned king of Italy. But a decade later, after establishing what he hoped to be a lasting peace, and perhaps thinking Arduin was a spent force, Henry departed to inspect other areas of his kingdom. Not one to miss an opportunity, Arduin attacked a city called Vercelli as soon as Henry's back was turned in the spring of 1014.

A few months prior to these events, Henry had been crowned Holy Roman Emperor by Pope Benedict VIII. The trouble with Arduin may have taken the shine off Henry's Imperial Coronation but the following year, Henry received good news. Arduin was taken ill and went off to live, somewhat ironically, as a monk. Then, towards the end of 1015, he died thus ending the career of a man who had been nothing but a nuisance.

The other main problem for Henry, both before and after his coronation as emperor, was Boleslaw. Up until 1018, their relationship continued in much the same vein with Henry carrying the fight to his erstwhile nemesis, marauding deep into Poland. Whilst the emperor did make gains, he also sustained significant losses. Peace agreements were made on more than one occasion and quickly broken off. However, the losses for both sides were not sustainable and Boleslaw also had his sights set on putting his son on the throne of Kiev. In 1018, Boleslaw finally recognised Henry as his overlord whilst Henry promised to help Boleslaw with his campaign into Kiev.

Also in 1018, Henry gained another success when the ageing ruler of Burgundy, Rudolf, made him his heir. Rudolf did so by declaring his intentions at a ceremony with all his nobility in attendance. To make sure of the deal, Rudolf swore an oath a second time. However, his plans were altered by the fact that Henry would die before him in 1024.

Towards the end of his work and also his own life, the chronicler Thietmar of Merseburg describes the generosity of Henry both to the church and to the poor. A ruler's relationship with the church would ultimately be the making or breaking of their reputation with chroniclers and Henry's seems to have not only been conventionally pious but ensured that the church in his kingdom was well maintained.

Henry also, like emperors before and after him, had a tetchy relationship with the Byzantine empire who controlled parts of Italy and was seeking to expand. He led an expedition to counter this particular threat which ultimately ended in very little progress and Henry died a couple of years later.

It's quite hard to sum up Henry as a ruler. Ultimately his reign, first as king of Germany and then as Emperor, was dominated by almost constant feuding with powerful enemies. Boleslaw's reputation does show that Henry was more than capable militarily however. Perhaps somewhat surprisingly, he had no heirs and given that his own succession was a contested one, it might well have proved wiser for him to do so.

Conrad II was born in the late 980s or early 990s to Henry, Count of Speyer and Adelaide of Metz, a French noblewoman. Conrad became Holy Roman Emperor in 1027, three years after the previous emperor had died. Henry II left the empire in good order but after his death things took a turn for the worse as instability set in and unscrupulous men sought to advance themselves during the uncertainty. Civil war was threatening to break and violence appeared to be about to rip the empire apart if it wasn't for powerful noblemen and Henry II's empress, a woman by the name of Cunigunde, intervening on behalf of the kingdom of Germany and the wider empire and putting a stop to any potential plots, coups and brutality. Despite their best efforts though, the kingdom needed a new figurehead. Henry had no heirs so the anxiety and uncertainty only increased.

So, with no clear candidate for the throne, the nobles came together to try and elect a new king. Many men threw their hat into the ring but for a variety of reasons, the options were soon whittled down quickly. Men were ruled out of the running for either being too old or too young; others, whilst perhaps being the right age, were still considered immature and not of the qualities required in a king whilst still more men were rejected for not having enough experience in battle, a major sticking point when it came to medieval kingship. Eventually, the options came down to two. Both men were called Conrad but of differing experience. Conrad The Younger was no older than 21 at the time of the election whilst his rival Conrad The Elder was significantly more experienced, aged now around 35. Cases for both men were put forward but Conrad The Elder, having put forward a lengthy and compelling speech, won enough support for election. Conrad The Younger accepted the outcome gracefully enough although men on his behalf, mainly from Lotharangia, were altogether less forgiving. After a brief period of mutiny, matters eventually settled down.

Conrad was consecrated king of Germany in September of 1024. By all accounts, it was a joyous occasion. According to Wipo of Burgundy, who wrote the Deeds of Conrad II, the people of Mainz, where the ceremony took place, were so ecstatic that even Charlemagne himself would not have received a better welcome. After the usual oaths and vows were sworn, incuding to forgive those who may have wronged Conrad in the past, Conrad was crowned and celebrated with a magnificent feast. Alongside the king was his wife Gisela who Wipo praises lavishly. Gisela was modest, humble, pious and of a noble spirit. She was a suitable companion for Conrad.

Conrad, from very early on in his reign, was diligent in his carrying out of his obligations to his people. He even demonstrated as such during his progress to his coronation. He was approached by a number of different men, all from humble origins and all with a grievance. The new king, despite advice from those around him, gave them his ear and set their affairs in order. Conrad was fully aware of the importance of public image and being seen to carry out justice fairly. He cleverly used these unexpected situations to enhance his own reputation in front of the common populace.